The 1000 Men Strong Leader

The Secret To Effortlessly Building A Network Marketing Empire

James Watson

© Copyright 2018 by James Watson

All rights reserved.

The following Book is reproduced below with the goal of providing information that is as accurate and reliable as possible. Regardless, purchasing this eBook can be seen as consent to the fact that both the publisher and the author of this book are in no way experts on the topics discussed within and that any recommendations or suggestions that are made herein are for entertainment purposes only. Professionals should be consulted as needed prior to undertaking any of the action endorsed herein.

This declaration is deemed fair and valid by both the American Bar Association and the Committee of Publishers Association and is legally binding throughout the United States.

Furthermore, the transmission, duplication or reproduction of any of the following work including specific information will be considered an illegal act irrespective of if it is done electronically or in print. This extends to creating a secondary or tertiary copy of the work or a recorded copy and is only allowed with express written consent from the Publisher. All additional right reserved.

The information in the following pages is broadly considered to be a truthful and accurate account of facts, and as such any inattention, use or misuse of the information in question by the reader will render any resulting actions solely under their purview. There are no scenarios in which the publisher or the original author of this work can be in any fashion deemed liable for any hardship or damages that may befall them after undertaking information described herein.

Additionally, the information in the following pages is intended only for informational purposes and should thus be thought of as universal. As befitting its nature, it is presented without assurance regarding its prolonged validity or interim quality. Trademarks that are mentioned are done without written consent and can in no way be considered an endorsement from the trademark holder.

Table of Contents

Introduction 6
Chapter 1: Getting Started in Network Marketing 7
    Investing in Your Future 7
    Network Marketing 8
    Well, what does it take to get started in network marketing? 9
        Gain some knowledge 9
    Believe that it will work for you 10
Chapter 2: Why Network Marketing? 12
    Advantages of a Network Marketing Income 12
    But have you asked yourself why Network Marketing? Here are a couple of facts for you 13
        It's Legal 13
        Most companies fail, few succeed 15
        Most Distributors call it quits before they can succeed 15
        We play a key role in the global economy as we grow 16
    It is real, and it works 16
    Why do companies do Network Marketing? 17
    But, why is it that most network marketers struggle? 17
Chapter 3: Demystifying Network Marketing Myths 20
    Clearing Up Myths About Network Marketing 21
    Can I succeed in Network Marketing if I work on a part-time basis? 21
    Is it a must to generate "Sales?" 22

Can I become a billionaire?...22

Is it a must to sponsor thousands of people to achieve success?.......23

Is NWM another get-rich-quick scheme?..23

If Network Marketing is such a great thing, why are we having just a few people participating in it?..23

I gave Network Marketing a shot, but it didn't go well for me..........24

I might not get the time to begin a Network Marketing business. I have a lot of things that I am already doing...24

Don't we have to join at the start to stand a chance of making real money? Doesn't NWM eventually get saturated?...................................25

Just a few people succeed in Network Marketing..............................25

Prospecting...27

Chapter 4: Choosing the right Company 31

Facts About Network Marketing..31

Four things that you must consider before you assess an NWM program 32

    Product..32

    Company...34

    Compensation Plan..35

Chapter 5: Building a Customer-Focused Selling 40

Sales..41

    The Prospective buyer..41

    Product or service being offered...41

    Make it simple and easy to buy..42

7 roles of Selling..42

The Art of Making Presentations..45

Two-On-Ones 45

Small Group Meetings 46

Open Meetings 47

Steps to follow to give an effective Network Marketing Presentation 47

Top 10 Proven tips in Network Marketing 50

Chapter 6: Lessons from A Network Marketing Millionaire 52

Let's start with the two-a-day concept 52

Make that choice to succeed 53

You are the Key 54

Keeping it real 55

The power of networking 55

Conclusion 56

Description 58

Introduction

Well, before we start, I want you to erase everything that you think you know about building a Network Marketing (NWM) Business. This book was written for all those people looking forward to making the world a much better place, and build massive wealth in the process. This could be the day that your life is going to change. You are about to learn how you can put your Network Marketing business in the right perspective so that you can get out and build a business of your dreams—a type of business that you are confident of building because you know that you have the right knowledge and steps on how to do it combined with the correct company.

The Network Marketing Industry has so much for both you and me! It can be the solution to millions of people in the world if it is treated correctly. I don't want you to miss anything. I want you to be part of a new wave of opportunity that Network Marketing provides. So get ready with a pen and notebook to jot down short notes.

To that end, the following chapters are going to help you get started with Network Marketing so that you know what you haven't been doing right. You will learn why this is the perfect time to get into Network Marketing, and what unique benefits Network Marketing provides. The book shall further demystify popular Network Marketing myths, and take you through the game of prospecting and how you can master the art of prospecting that is very key in Network Marketing.

We present to you the blueprints of choosing the right company. You will learn the art of building a customer-focused selling and the top 10 proven tips that every successful Network Marketing professional has followed. Lastly, you get the chance to learn lessons from a prominent Network Marketing Millionaire who has been recruiting 30 new people every month into his company for the last ten years.

Chapter 1: Getting Started in Network Marketing

Since the inception of the Industrial Revolution nearly 250 years ago, the concept of a career has been that you have to work for at least 40 hours a week for a minimum of 40 years before you can generate 40% of what was never sufficient for the first 40 years.

The required path to follow was:

1. Get a four-year degree in your pocket.
2. Search for a good job with a big reputable company.
3. Get the job.
4. Work for next 40 years before you retire and enjoy your prime years.

A lot of things have changed since then. For instance, your company is likely to have decided to file for bankruptcy as a way to escape paying your retirement salary. This does not only happen to companies. States, cities, and counties have started to realize that they overpromised and can't fulfill their promises. Therefore, they resort to filing for bankruptcy as a means to escape their health and retirement duties. Well, whether the retirement was there or not, you will realize that there is barely enough revenue from this idea to sustain you in your golden years. In fact, you will discover that people end up running out time. Perhaps one reason for this could be that they think there are many chances to get another shot at it.

Investing in Your Future

It is one of the key secrets of building a successful career. Did you know that many Tech companies today are tapping on kids aged 16-20 years old to create products? Several companies have rolled up startups to teach and nurture talents in young children.

All things constant, going to college makes you smarter than not going to college. But, there are certain college kids that are discovering that if they can dedicate those four full years to improving their ideas, talents, and businesses, they might finally come to recruit many college graduates. For a few seconds, stop reading and just think about Steve Jobs, Larry Ellison, Mark Zuckerberg, and Bill Gates. What do they have in common? They all dropped out of college to continue building their income empires.

Despite the many young adults who stick to the college model and get jobs at the end of their career, they are also burdened with the duty to clear large school loans. This type of debt is very depressing to most people since they can't afford to pay it off. In an ideal world, if your goal is to become a lawyer, doctor, or engineer, going an extra level in your education is better. However, there are better options for those who don't want to follow that route. Maybe you could be the next Mark Zuckerberg. Who knows?

Network Marketing

It could be that it is your first time and you would want to know how you can get started in network marketing. Or maybe you already have involved yourself in network marketing, but due to some circumstances, you got stuck on the way, and now you want to find out how you can get started again. Or perhaps you fall into the third category of those people already in network marketing, and only want to discover how they can keep improving.

Well, in the same way, I believed that network marketing was far too easy to get started, I still believe that today it is more difficult than it is. In fact, if you are thinking of getting started in network marketing, for sure you must understand that most people never build a network marketing empire in one year—not even in two years, three years, or four years.

But you can. Why? This book is about building your Network marketing empire. Our tagline is "Yes, you can!" We take you on a complete journey and show you the right way to follow.

Well, what does it take to get started in network marketing?

When you know that you are struggling to fulfill your monthly needs or even make ends meet, it becomes really difficult to justify your expenses, especially if you are not generating any money—like so many people out there who have joined a network marketing company but don't know how to keep going or what steps to take to become successful. Here are some steps to help you get the ball rolling on network marketing.

Gain some knowledge

Most importantly, you need to get informed or educated with at least some obvious things that will help you build and run a network marketing business. That is actually what you are already doing, and that's why you are here today.

In the past, while starting out as a young employee, I got a job with a company that had one of the best training programs. By working in this company, I went on to expand my skills and became a professional marketing consultant. Since then, I have made use of that training, not only in network marketing but in all spheres of my life.

A few years ago, my view of companies was mainly based on publicity, often about their pay plans. Today, when I look at it, I laugh at how foolish it all was. And this is what I mean: you can create the most attractive pay plan ever to be created, but if there is no one doing anything, it follows that no one is going to make money too.

There are so many services and products unveiled in the market today, all released by different network marketing companies. But, how do you really tell which one to choose?

Well, do you recall the name of the movie with actors Billy Crystal and Jack Palance? If you don't, I will help you out. It was called "City Slickers!" It is a movie that will crack your ribs because of its hilarious comedy. Still, in that particular movie, there is a scene where Curly asks Mitch, played by Billy Crystal, "Do you know what the secret of life is?" Mitch looks at Curly. Curly goes ahead to raise up one finger and says, "This!" Mitch asks, "your finger?" Curly replies, "One thing. Just one thing. You stick to that, and the rest don't mean shit!" Surprised, Mitch asks again, "but what is that one thing?" Curly smiles and replies "That's what you have to find out!"

I find this part of the movie as having the most thought-provoking statements that you can apply to your life today! The last two statements are very powerful. What highlights can you draw from that? Most of us have perhaps heard most people say, "find something that you are passionate about, and you will never think of it as work!" Getting started and running a network marketing company is work.

So will it be sensible to identify something you would love to do? Something you like? And then carry out your own little research to see if there is a network marketing company that offers the same?

Believe that it will work for you

We said earlier that our tagline is "Yes, you can," and there is nothing that describes this point than the belief that it will work for you and anyone you will offer. Just one thing to remember is that this would take a bit of time. However, it plays the most key aspect of figuring out. Don't forget that it is "success that comes from belief "and not "belief from success."

I know that most of the rules that we grew up with have continuously been forgotten and thrown out of the window as years pass by. But, having one job is no longer safe. The average person today can switch jobs about seven to ten times in their lifetime. Most people begin to save or invest when their children are out of college or when they are into their late fifties. However, if you are going to begin saving and investing at the age of 50, it means you only have approximately 20 years of accumulation. The most important thing you need to put into consideration when it comes to saving and investing is not how much you are investing, but for what period.

That said, if there is one thing that I have come to learn over the last 5 years about building an income generating source, it is the truth that you must be ready to lead on the front instead of leading from the tail end. I know that many of us have been caught at the tail end on many different occasions. But, believing that it is going to work for you is the chance for you to create your own wealth and become the next millionaire. Pick on new trends and lead by example. The Network Marketing community consists of people who are ready to pounce on the next trends long before anyone notices them.

Key points

In short, if you are getting started in Network Marketing you must:

1. Be ready to seek knowledge
2. Believe it will work for you
3. Invest in your future

Chapter 2: Why Network Marketing?

Network marketing is about creating something from nothing. Just like "Free Enterprise." It is the least and simplest way for any ordinary individual to begin living an extraordinary life. But don't get me wrong when I say "living extraordinarily." I simply mean living a rich life—not getting rich. To live a rich life, you must get concerned with who you become rather than what you accumulate. The old saying that "money can never buy happiness" is very true. Your goal should be to live an excellent life and money should be an added flavor.

Advantages of a Network Marketing Income

1. You have the chance to build it passively.

2. You have complete freedom to build it from whichever place you want.

3. You can unveil it for a minimum of $500.

4. The business you are running is for yourself rather than by yourself. This implies that it is your host company that must carry out all the heavy investing involved.

5. All your business partners including the senior ones in your network have a specific personal interest in your success. There is someone on your team that is working to make sure it succeeds, and they want something better other than motivating and teaching you so that it works for you.

6. You have the time and freedom for you to develop tax deductions every year.

7. There is that opportunity to learn while you earn. A possibility exists for creating cash flow in your first month.

8. Still, you have the opportunity to begin earning an extra $500 or even more each month so that you can invest in other options.

9. As time goes on, success in your business will be generated for you by more than thousands of people who shall be creating their own success through building an asset income. This means that the cycle could continue forever no matter whether you are working hard on it or simply resting. A genuine asset income will always create a net worth.

If you don't know, the net worth of your Network Marketing income could go up to by $2000 of your monthly income. This means that if your monthly residual asset income is approximately $4,000, your net worth income could be close to $1 million. Well, can you calculate how much you require to earn and invest so that you raise $1 million in equities? What about the duration? How much would you require to sacrifice before you can achieve it?

As you can see, asset income helps you build your net worth much faster whereby you can achieve your target net worth in a span of five to ten years.

But have you asked yourself why Network Marketing? Here are a couple of facts for you.

It's Legal

Let's take for example, in more than 70 countries across the world, Network Marketing has been legally applied to distribute products and compensate distributors for over 50 years. During this period, the federal and state courts have been supporting Network Marketing as a viable distribution and compensation method when the following legal guidelines adhere:

A. The primary objective of the business is to sell legal services or products at a market price. What this means is that there should be a market for the product from consumers without financial opportunity. So the test is simple. Do you have customers that are ready to purchase the product without any link to the Network Marketing door? Is the product real and at an affordable price, or is it another type of money game?

B. There is no promise for prospective incomes. This is not a fair playing field like other business worlds. Even Sports-betting companies and lotteries hype us to think that we can win big prices. So, be careful of Network Marketing companies that promise high income without any proof.

C. Distributors don't necessarily require to be paid for recruiting other people. The income is entirely generated from the sale of products.

There are many types of products and services that distributors can act as customers as long as they have the financial power to purchase it. As you can see that the means justify the end. However, when every good thing about a product is exhausted, no one wants to use it. It then turns out that this was a pyramid scheme. But, the real test of a genuine Network Marketing company is if the product is still sold to consumers not earning any royalties or commissions from the opportunities. The majority of the Network Marketing distributors begin by looking for the opportunity to earn income, but once they quit they choose to become a customer. Most total sales for companies are from "wholesale" customers. This accounts for about 70% of most Network Marketing sales forces. The remaining 30% is made up of those that earn maybe a few hundred to a few thousand per month.

Most companies fail, few succeed

In the U.S there are approximately 2,000 Network Marketing companies that distribute over $30 billion every year in goods and services. Among this, less than 300 are Direct Selling Association members. We have few successful and legitimate firms that aren't DSA members for reasons unknown. Often, DSA membership is among the highest standards of legal and ethical scrutiny. Usually, DSA member companies have already gone through a rigorous vetting process.

In many cases, you will discover that most Network Marketing firms don't make it. Most hotels and restaurant don't prosper. The majority of the dry cleaners together with companies that we went to work for immediately after finishing college failed. But, there are some that still flourish. For instance, Herbalife, Forever Living Products, Mary Kay, Usana and Nu Skin are multi-billion dollar companies and have been in business for many years. That is the nature of free markets and enterprise.

Most Distributors call it quits before they can succeed

Some lucky Distributors have tested and experienced the fortunes of a long-standing asset royalty income of more than $1 million every year for many years. There are elite business creators who, after investing between 5 to 10 years, start to earn income in the range of $25,000-$100,000 per month. However, most earn in the range of $1,000 to $10,000 per month while the masses earn a few hundred dollars. And don't forget that these are people that did not give up along the way.

Most people who get started with building a Network Marketing business give up along the way before they can even achieve the level of success for which they wanted. Many average network marketers don't create enough opportunities beyond purchasing a product at wholesale. For sure, the truth is that individuals with average ambitions, dedication, and effort often don't go far in business such as Network Marketing.

Well, do you think this is the fault of the individual or system? Both, that is what I think. Network Marketing is not like shooting fish in a barrel. Who do you know today who is planning to get started in Network Marketing? Maybe you are because you are already involved. To succeed in Network Marketing profession, you must have a certain degree of personal confidence, develop an interest to speak to people, get comfortable building new relationships every day, be ready to learn, and most importantly, be an active leader of the Network Marketing profession.

We play a key role in the global economy as we grow

Did you know that the Network Marketing method of marketing has been growing for the past 20 years? This includes 90% in the last 10 years. Over $110 billion worth of goods and services are always sold across the world every year in this industry. Nearly close to 500,000 people across the world become sales representatives every week for one of these firms. About 67 million people across the world take part in this concept.

More than 30 years ago, there were no written books or blogs on the topic of Network Marketing. Today there are many copies. In fact, some have sold millions of copies. Twenty years ago there was no mainstream magazines or television shows that featured the positive motivation opportunity in the industry of Network Marketing. Now, you can find hundreds of examples. Twenty years ago, you could never find a mentor or a leader that endorsed this profession. Today, dozens of them do. There are thousands of firms and millions of sales representatives each with the one focus on building their team. This idea has rapidly grown, and it's about to blow up in a good way.

It is real, and it works

The bottom line is that Network Marketing is real and it works. A few successful people have used it to build extraordinary personal wealth for over 60 years. In fact, the smartest people in the world have taken advantage of it.

Why do companies do Network Marketing?

Well, now you know some crucial facts about network marketing. Do you? And do you know why a lot of companies decide to do network marketing? Here's why. Have you ever thought that the cost acquisition of finding a customer is very cheap? Look. This is what I mean. I don't need to go and create a T.V ad and spend $500,000. I simply get that done at a very low price and find somebody to go sell it while I can pay extra to the field. But, there's a good reason why most people choose to do network marketing. And that is because the cost of getting a customer is cheaper.

But, why is it that most network marketers struggle?

I have attended several Network Marketing training events. However, one thing that amuses me is the way almost everybody in attendance approaches their business or starts it in the wrong way. I can't blame these people for doing this. Why? Do you know that Network Marketing is all about emulating and working as well as learning from what your seniors are doing? And so these people are simply doing what they have learned. This is what makes it a duplicate. Well, I got tired of this type of approach. It is an old style of network marketing that chances of getting successful are very minimal.

The absence of key business knowledge is the primary reason for why many people struggle. It's very sad. So many people in this profession fail to reach their goals even if they were to follow or listen what experts say or do. Regardless of how much training you attend, if you don't have the fundamental knowledge, then you will still struggle. I'm going to talk about the issues I have seen and experienced. I believe that my unique perspective on past experiences has the potential to make a very big difference in your business. I am not going to sit on the sidelines and continue to watch as many businesses fail to attain their projected goals because of the lack of key knowledge of how to run a successful network marketing business.

Before we can move on to demystify some of the networking marketing myths, I want to take a few minutes to help align your network marketing profession and business into the correct perspective. I want you to begin to see and create a mind map of how it appears in the larger market of "business." Most importantly, we delve into how the networking marketing business has been implemented for the last fifty years, currently, and where the present state of network marketing is going and how it's about to change.

Did you know that having knowledge and understanding of the current position of Network Marketing profession is crucial to your future success? I am going to demonstrate to you the biggest contributing factor for why this profession has lagged behind much more than it is expected and for much longer than it should have. Later, we shall look at tips to use to avoid some of these obstacles and begin to count profits.

I am going to keep everything simple so that you have an easy time to read and conceptualize. So let's start! In any kind of business, whenever you want to go and market, promote your product or service, most of the time you take time to research and find out something about your target audience. Here we are going to take the example the of the alcohol industry. Common sense has it that you won't be walking in the marketplace trying to convince people who do not take alcohol to buy it. You would also not try to convince people who do not take alcohol to begin drinking. Most likely that is their choice or lifestyle to do so.

Well, now let's assume that for the last fifty years, alcohol companies rolled a marketing plan to convince these non-alcohol drinkers to start taking alcohol, and went ahead to convince them that they should purchase their quality drink. You will agree with me that the whole alcohol industry would develop a very bad reputation. Well, while this example looks ridiculous, I have picked on it because I want you to see exactly where most network marketers have been getting it wrong for the last fifty years. All along they have been trying to address the wrong type of audience. Now, do you think this is a smart move? Of course not! Listen to me carefully.

This is apparently why many people across the world have this perception that if you are involved in a network marketing business, that is a scam or a pyramid scheme. It is for the same reason that you see people with smart ideas and hopes fail to give a shot in network marketing. This is outrageously shameful! Sometimes I ask myself how many seven-figure earners or six-figure earners out there would have experienced huge success in Network Marketing, building great companies and helping so many people out there do the same, but failed to get that opportunity. Now, it is my goal to change that and let this book do its job of erasing that preconceived false notion of NWM.

Key Points

1. Knowledge is key to the success of Network Marketing
2. Understanding your target market plays a big role in successful Network Marketing.
3. Many businesses struggle to succeed because of insufficient knowledge.
4. Network Marketing is real.

Chapter 3: Demystifying Network Marketing Myths

Many people like to ask me to tell them the big secrets to success. Part of the reason is that I have had the opportunity to work with hundreds of highly successful people in finance and business, and the good news is that there are no big secrets to success. Think of it this way: if indeed it was true that there were secrets to success, would that secret be still a secret today? How many people would have been successful? I guess nearly everyone would have been successful? But again, the big question remains, how could the world be with everyone successful?

There are a few tools that when used correctly, the end goal is that you find a way in life. Frequently Asked Questions(FAQ) is one of those most effective tools used in NWM today. It saves a lot of time for you, and it acts as a massive learning tool for your organization. Whether you have laid down plans to build your network business offline or online, one of the most important things you should consider to do is to prepare and create an FAQ document and ensure that every member in your organization has a copy of the document. To distribute it online, just make it accessible on your company website. For offline purposes, have the document in your folders or files.

You know very well that responding to the same questions every day consumes much of our valuable time. Therefore, answering questions quickly and in an accurate manner for your online and offline distributors is key to achieving success in network marketing business. When you have a readily available softcopy and hardcopy of your FAQ document, then you make it easy for your potential distributors to access it.

I know you might not know this—people quickly remember what

they have read rather than what they have heard—so by creating an FAQ document, not only will you save time for yourself, but you will also help them remember the answers to their questions. Well, I know you could be asking yourself this question. How can I develop an FAQ document? Don't worry. Here are the things to look out for:

- Try to ask yourself what questions you had in mind when you first started your company.
- Consider the most frequently asked questions from your prospect distributors.
- Find out whether the questions they are asking have been answered anywhere in the company training resources. If yes, then in your FAQ, give them directions on where to go and read the answers.
- Keep updating your FAQ when you get unique questions that aren't answered in it.

Clearing Up Myths About Network Marketing

If you still experience problems with the right way to develop an FAQ document, use this template.

Can I succeed in Network Marketing if I work on a part-time basis?

Yes, the choice is in your hands. You can choose to start your NWM business on a part-time basis without interfering with your main source of income. Aside from this, you can also decide to operate your business on a part-time basis. What you should know is that the majority of men and women in the Network Marketing Industry operate their business passively.

Is it a must to generate "Sales?"

I will suggest that you respond to this with a question rather than a normal response. You can ask, "Do you prefer sales?" If the person answers yes, then you can say something like, "You will obviously like this!" However, if the person says no, then again you can answer with, "You'll obviously love this!" As you can see, this sounds unclear, but the fact is that NWM takes both sides of the coin.

Network marketing consists of selling a service or product. Therefore, one can refer to it as sales. But, the traditional sales method of transactions has to complete once you purchase the product or service. Then, the salesperson turns to the next prospect. This is not the same with networking. In NWM, purchasing a product or receiving a certain service is the start of a long-term business relationship. So you can see that this is nowhere near sales. In short, what I am trying to say is that Network Marketing is a conversational type of business which is about you sharing the product and concept of an NWM company that you enjoy to use and love.

Can I become a billionaire?

Well, this is certainly difficult to answer, but for sure I can't be able to tell. However, what I can suggest is that you ask yourself how much would you want to earn. How much effort are you willing to put in to realize your target goal? Remember, no limit has been set for you when it comes to NWM industry. It is only regulated by a well-known cliché "the sky's the limit" and how fast you can reach it.

You will reap what you sow. Don't expect to be a billionaire if you aren't doing the effort needed to become a billionaire. If you target to earn little, you will earn that little; target much, and you will receive that much, as long as you work. I want you to look at it this way. The income you raise in your Network Marketing is just residual. This means that you have the opportunity to earn even more not just for today alone, but for the rest of the remaining years.

Is it a must to sponsor thousands of people to achieve success?

No. You don't need to do so. In fact, you don't require to sponsor anyone. If you like, you can develop a retail business. Don't forget that you do whatever you're comfortable with. While you can still generate some good income with retail, building a marketing company or organization gives you the chance to generate a huge amount of money. If you are to go and operate a retail business alone, then that business will control you.

Conversely, if you choose to hire at least one or two persons within a month into your company or organization, you have the greatest potential to build a large organization. By sponsoring more people in your organization, you help increase the number of products that will spread through your Multi-Level Marketing (MLM) business. And this increases your rewards exponentially.

Is NWM another get-rich-quick scheme?

Well, let me first clear this false misconception. There is never anything like "get-rich-quick." The same way there is no secret to success besides working smart and hard. For anything that has value, it takes time to create. It is very rare to find anything that does not obey that rule. In fact, if you ever dreamt of getting rich overnight, maybe you better try to play the lottery. Still, you might not win the lottery no matter how many times you play.

If Network Marketing is such a great thing, why are we having just a few people participating in it?

Think about this. If surgeons and lawyers earn a lot of money, why can't we have more than 20,000,000 people working in those professions in your country? We can sum that in one word: a misconception. The general public has a limited understanding of the concept of Network Marketing. However, this perception has, in the recent years, started to change quickly. There are no exact reasons to explain why the public seems to have this wrong misconception. Maybe it could be they seek advice from the wrong people, friends, or co-workers on how to become wealthy. Maybe they haven't encountered someone who can discuss with them the real facts of NWM. Again, don't forget that people have that freedom to do what they want. There are some who have set priorities, and maybe watching a soccer or basketball game every night is their first priority over securing financial freedom.

I gave Network Marketing a shot, but it didn't go well for me.

No problem! You could be the obstacle. Do you remember when you were starting to learn how to walk while you were a young kid? You probably had to fall down several times before you finally started to at least walk a few steps forward. Probably, you were disappointed when you couldn't generate wealth overnight. Sometimes, this doesn't take place. Researchers call it delayed gratification. Remember that even a farmer never plants seeds today and expect to harvest the next day in the morning. Network Marketing is like planting seeds. There is no difference. You must be willing to be patient. There are reputable Network Marketing companies, fair NWM companies, and then there are some that are bad and unfair. But NWM still works! You only need to find the right marketing company.

I might not get the time to begin a Network Marketing business. I have a lot of things that I am already doing.

Did you know why you should consider NWM? There is no other

reason other than getting that financial freedom to do all the things in life that you would want to do. That extra time you need can never run away and hide under the bed or carpet. If you find NWM worth it for you, no matter how busy you are in life, you will still squeeze in that little time to build your NWM business. If you say that you don't have the time now, do you think you will ever get that time? I request you make the time now rather than waiting for the right time.

Don't we have to join at the start to stand a chance of making real money? Doesn't NWM eventually get saturated?

This is yet another popular misconception spread by the media and inexperienced people. First, saturation has never happened in Network Marketing. Secondly, Network Marketing is yet to achieve the exact growth, and that is because there are millions of potential individuals who are yet to hear of Network Marketing. And it might take decades for one to fix this.

But wait. Here is the main reason why Network Marketing getting saturated is a myth. There are thousands of new prospects opened every month. This figure has young adults that have attained that stage where they would like to start a business. Then we have a certain figure that has experienced a tremendous change in their lives either because of changes at home, work, etc. These are the same people who, a few months ago, no one considered as prospects for NWM, and suddenly they are embracing the opportunity. The truth that I want you to know today is that NWM is wide open with many opportunities.

Just a few people succeed in Network Marketing

Well, the most unfortunate thing with nature is that not many succeed in any industry. Most individuals will never do what it takes to reap the benefits of Network Marketing. NWM is all about the effort you put in. Many people get it wrong when they join NWM with the notion that this is the easiest way to get rich. That is not true. You must be ready to sweat. A lot of people simply want to earn money that they haven't worked for and give up when they are unable to get it. Most of these people are the ones you will hear saying "I gave it a shot for two weeks and it didn't work. It's just a scam!" You cannot lay the blame on NWM, but it is yourself to blame.

What does the average person often do? They throw in the towel at anything they attempt. Approximately 90% of young small businesses fail to go past the fourth year, and the owners bid goodbye with a few thousand dollars that an average NWM person invests! The most interesting thing about NWM is that it is very easy to get into, and at the same time very easy to get out.

This is usually a genuine business, and one has to approach it as a genuine business—one that you have put in your life asset. Think of it this way, if you were an eye optician, and you have invested $20,000 in equipment to start an eye clinic, not factoring in more than $20,000 and all the years you dedicated to getting that degree, you would perhaps continue to hang in there until the time the clinic starts to generate good income because you invested a lot of money to simply give up!

Well, that's what you need to do in Network Marketing. You have to dedicate your time and continue working until the time you make it work. Sometimes because of the low income, you require getting started. Some people don't take it seriously. Instead, they treat it as a hobby. If only you could take some time and look at NWM from the big picture, then I believe you would never treat it like any other common business. Most people who want to get started in NWM give up even before they start. Some quit in the first week when they discover the amount of effort and commitment involved.

However, the few people who have the determination, drive, and vision to dedicate most of their time and efforts to do what it takes to eat the fruits of NWM succeed! So don't lay the blame on Network Marketing model. Who should you blame? The person involved.

Prospecting

Paul Myer once said that it doesn't matter the level of success you have attained or how much skills you have amassed. If you encounter a person who has mastered the art of prospecting, you will for sure be beaten pants down. Well, prospecting is a disciplined form of art. It can be a game, a science of sales, or even psychology. And lastly, it can also be a very competitive event. Like all forms of art, mastering the art of prospecting requires practice, coaching, and training. And just like all other arts, you can only be a master by practicing again and again. Network Marketers who are crowned as masters of the game are our main key business winners. And if you are still wondering how you can be a master of prospecting, here is how you start.

Do you know how gold was traditionally excavated? Usually, the gold miners had to dig in the prospected gold site and endure the tons of dust before they could find an ounce of gold. Often, these people didn't care much about the dust because they knew what they are after is much more valuable compared to the dust and efforts they are putting in.

Prospecting is similar to traditional gold miners. You have the chance to amass an abundance of wealth and success in life if you just master and learn the rules of prospecting. While attempting to follow this path, you are going to face many different challenges. But if you hold on and continue to search for the ounce of gold, I can assure you that you will get it one day.

In NWM, gold is an embodiment of those leaders that will help you discover your path to unlimited wealth. As long as you maintain that focus and determination, you will get more people than you can manage. Remember, if it is your first time in NWM, out of 100 phone calls you are going to make, you are going to reach 50, and you will schedule an appointment with 25. However, while you continue to gain experience, your ratio will get better. Therefore, the secret to building a Network Marketing Empire is to deliver your message to a large target audience in an efficient, elaborate, and effective way. Let me narrate to you a short story related to prospecting.

In a certain town, there lived two little boys who traveled to the market to sell carpets. Since the market was far from where they lived, the two boys used a donkey to travel to the market. Before they could arrive at the market, one of the boys said to the other, "You will go and sell your carpets near the entrance to the market, and I will go stand on the other side, just to make sure that we don't miss on any buyer."

As the sun kept on rising, many traders walked in and out of the entrance. At times, a passer-by would stop and ask the boy who stood at the entrance of the market, "How much do you sell your carpet?" The boy would then give a response. When the sun was about to set, the two little boys closed their business and met up and went home on their donkey. On the way home, the boy who stood at the entrance asked the other, "How much carpets did you manage to sell?" He replied, "None! Nobody came to ask me for anything." His friend had mercy on him and consoled him, "I will take that position tomorrow, and you will take my front position. Being at the front might give you some good opportunities to sell some before dawn arrives."

Early in the morning the two little boys climbed on the donkey with their carpets and headed to the market. They arrived and, as agreed on yesterday, they exchanged their positions. Evening came and the two boys prepared to return home. The boy who stood at the exit of the market asked his friend, "Well, how many carpets did you manage to sell today?" Frowning and feeling disgraced replied, "Not even one my friend, no one came to ask for any carpets today, I seem to be very unlucky. What should I do?" Struck by surprise, his friend asked, "Are you serious? You didn't even sell one? I thought you had the best location to help you sell at least five carpets!"

The unlucky boy said, "Yes, passers-by just passed as if I didn't sell anything. No one stopped by to speak or ask me anything." It was a long journey, and so when they arrived home, they looked for a place to rest. The other boy tried to find out how the unlucky boy carried out his sales. After many hours of trying to figure out why the other boy rarely sold a single carpet in two days, they found out that the boy was unlucky for the last two days because not only he did not stand there the entire day, but he also never displayed his items, and so nobody knew what he was selling or why he stood there!

Well, while this story might sound funny and at the same time ironic, the lesson that we can draw from here is that if you are looking forward to more success in the Network Marketing Industry, one must understand that this business calls for a lot of advertising. And that advertising can only be delivered by yourself. You need to tell everyone so that they stay informed of the type of business you are in. Some people think that prospects will come for them, and so they wait for very long as shown in the picture below.

Key points

1. Preparing a list of FAQs is the key to getting involved in Networking business.

2. FAQs save you time and speak volumes about your product and services.

3. Prospecting is all about meeting new people who can help you expand your business.

Chapter 4: Choosing the right Company

The primary key to achieving success in Network Marketing is finding the right company for yourself. There are hundreds of company to select from. At first, nearly all the companies seem to have good opportunities. If you already found a company that you want to get started with, this chapter will help you tell whether you have chosen the right company. If you are yet to settle for the right company, this chapter will offer you tips to pick the right choice. Before we start on selecting the right company, let's go through some facts.

Facts About Network Marketing

Are you aware that Network Marketing companies aren't different from the rest of other firms? They have a defined survival time frame. New companies venturing into any type of business have a great challenge of making it through the first few years. Many MLM companies will rise, but only a few will survive the turbulent storms until the second year. Then very few will go past five years.

There could be several reasons why a company might fail. Some companies might not be properly managed, some might be poorly financed, others might not have a well-designed product, and some may fail to be innovative, or some were shut down because of corrupt dealings. Surprisingly, when the company fails, the people who used to promote the same companies never come out to speak the real facts that led to the collapse of the company. But you deserve to know both the dark and bright side of the story. No one wants to get associated with a company that will finally fail. You want a company where your money, time, dreams, goals and most importantly your reputation are highly guarded.

The most critical thing that determines whether you will attain success in NWM is understanding the fact that NWM needs time and sometimes five years before you achieve total financial freedom. Complete financial freedom involves having the time to do something else without worrying about meeting your monthly obligations.

Four things that you must consider before you assess an NWM program

There are about four things that you must consider before you assess an NWM program: Company, Compensation Plan, Product, and Training Support. You can call them as the four engines of Network Marketing. Each one of these must be considered carefully before you get started. Let's look at each of them.

Product

When it comes to product assessment, the first thing that you must consider is the uniqueness of the product or service. Consider also the price of the product. The key features of products that succeed in NWM include:

- What is the emotional appeal of the service or product?
- Is the product unique, such that you are the only provider?
- If the product isn't completely unique, are you able to create a unique selling tagline to differentiate it from the completion?
- Does the price generate value and interest at the consumer level?
- Is it the price competitive?
- What are some of the customer advantages when he or she buys the product? Is there any customer money back guarantee just in case the customer feels unsatisfied with the product?

- In which way is the product training extensive for distributors?
- Does the company have the ability to expand the product as well as the services to the international and national levels?
- What are some of the main focus areas of the company? Is it hiring more people? Or creating innovative products and services?
- Does the company have good resources that describe their products?

Most of the time you will have to be a good customer of your own. You must learn to create your own sense of love for the product. Unless you become creative and develop a way that you love the product, you will find it very hard to recommend the product to potential customers. Imagine if Steve Jobs used Android phones, yet he is the one who invented the iPhone. That will show that he doesn't trust his own product. This can extensively affect the sales of the company.

As somebody who is just starting out and would like to build a Network Marketing empire, here are products that I can suggest you start with:

- Personal care products
- Nutritional supplements
- Weight loss and management
- Skin-care
- Jewelry
- Telecommunications services
- Books and educational products
- Internet-based services
- Household cleaning services

- Insurance products
- Make-up and beauty products

There are many other product categories which can fit in the above list. Just make sure that the product meets the consumer needs.

Company

This is the next engine that we look at: a great company is one that is financially strong. Once you are ready and feel comfortable to represent the product line, next is to perform a little research on the company's management, background, and philosophy. Of the three, the most important is the philosophy of the company.

If you're about to join a company that you don't have much information about, then you need to be careful because many people have been deceived in the past. You will encounter or discover that many of start-up companies have big claims concerning the provision of opportunities in the initial stage. Well, despite there being benefits in the initial stage, there is still a high level of risk. Most of the initial stages don't have sufficient materials for you to distribute or read. This means that you might not distribute your products or services in a timely manner. This becomes an immediate turn off to most people that you bring into your company.

Companies that have just started tend to experience multiple problems such as cash flow problems. For instance, your incentive cheque might not be ready on time. Because of such issues, I will advise that you confirm the financial stability and reputation of a company first. You need to be very sure that the company has solved 99% of their problems.

I have, over the past, come to learn and believe that the only thing that can ensure proper functioning of an NWM company is the level of experience of the management that runs the company—specifically, the CEO of the company.

The CEO is always among the first people you need to check out. Find out more about their experience with Network Marketing and as well as their knowledge. You really want that person who can help you reach your financial destination without much problems along the way. Here are some questions to help you judge the credibility of a company.

- Who are the directors of the company?
- Are the directors professionally certified to run the company?
- What about the commitment level of the CEO? What is his vision? Does he have plans of building a lifetime business?
- Does the company have enough staff to help run the company smoothly?
- Is the company management staff working towards a common goal?
- Who designed the company recognition programme?

You need to conduct a little research to find out each of the above-highlighted questions because you are making one of the most critical business decisions in your life. Remember that you will be investing your reputation, money, time and efforts in the business. If you believe that it is necessary to spend quality time searching for your mate—like I do—then the same energy should be applied in this particular decision. If you pick the right company, you stand the chance to change lives of thousands of people while also changing your own.

Compensation Plan

The third engine is the Compensation Plan. Payouts become meaningless if the products and services aren't of good quality. A well-implemented compensation plan can deliver a lifetime income for the people working on it. However, it is never easy for a new person to conceptualize all the complexities that a plan requires. However, it's still possible to identify some key traits found in the best plans. So, you should look at the following aspects when you are assessing a compensation plan:

- Exponential growth factor
- Fairness
- The distinction between reward and recognition
- The nominal levels in a pay-out
- Balance
- Rewards in proportion to the effort

Balance

You need to ensure that there exists some balance between the rewards you receive for personal selling and the sales generated by your downline network. It is important that you focus on both elements of your personal group. This means that you need to continue to sponsor people who work on the front line as well as those working deeper down the line.

Reward proportional to the effort

You need to have a clear link between reward and effort. This is important during the early stages of a business. Like the way many people prefer to say, there should be evidence that justice is achieved. This also applies to NWM.

As you slowly build your business, your rewards will mainly be useful at finding more people, training them, and giving them the support they need, as well sending a message of encouragement to help them develop within your network line. Still, the link shall exist between reward and effort.

Fairness

Your plan should be fair. It should not reward only recruiters with huge networks, but also it should consider distributors that have started in business or are in the stages of growth. Most of the time, plans that pay a large amount of money on different levels have the price of the product set high to help meet those rewards. This has the potential to bring down the sales because retail prices are too high for potential customers to purchase.

In other cases, there are plans which offer a reward to people because of their persistence to not throw in the towel. Regardless of what the distributors do, certain plans will double the size of the reward over a given time interval. You just need to remain patient, and soon you will find yourself at the top, no matter the level of merit!

Nominal pay-outs levels

Companies should have the ability to cover costs such as research and development, staff salaries, and other support services like quick data processing. There is no need to have a compensation plan that pays out a very large percentage but threatens the financial stability of the company. What if the company collapses? Will the people earn anything?

Exponential growth factor

Once you have your business attaining the critical mass, then leverage takes action through training others and sponsoring, and your rewards should rapidly increase. In short, this is a type of business where you are going to get paid a little cash for your initial effort, then finally you are going to get paid more for the little effort once your network grows.

What is the difference between reward and recognition?

A lot of plans seem to confuse the two words. Rewards should be awarded for the results. The ultimate result in MLM is the sales volume. This can either be through the wholesale or retail sales. Results usually reflect the productive activity one has put in. Therefore, nobody should just receive a reward because a given activity does not translate into results. Activity needs to be identified via non-monetary means like badges, pins, certificates and so on. This means that you should search for a compensation plan that comes with advancement incentives with a given motive before you concentrate on increasing the sales volume. This will also help sustain the members of your organization so that they continue to move forward. If you spot a compensation plan that is equally distributed as well as multidimensional, then you should know that you are finding a good opportunity.

Training Support

Correct and effective training is essential. We said somewhere that Network Marketing companies are similar to the rest of other normal companies. However, there exists only a little distinction. Similarly, Network Marketing is really just like any other genuine business out there. And in all genuine businesses, one must know how to run the operations of the business in the right way. Otherwise, you should forget all hopes of generating any money.

The NWM company should incorporate the following training programs:

- Product training
- Leadership training
- New Training for distributors
- Business building training

Some of these training sessions can get very intense. Other programs of the weekend such as motivating the distributors, improving their presentation skills, as well as boosting their public speaking skills can be very useful as time goes on. I was once a trainer, and I understand the need for training, and how it can make someone become effective after being trained several times. The same way you can recharge your phone regularly, training is no different. You have to empower your distributors time after time so that they discharge their duties efficiently.

Based on the many years I worked as a trainer, I have come to believe that individuals that receive training grow 90% faster than those who didn't. Often, training sharpens an individual and brings the best of the person. However, people who ignore training and look at it as if it a time-waster usually face many different problems when it comes to expanding the borders of their Network Marketing business. Many NWM companies are aware of the power of training, but very few companies are ready to set aside some money and provide effective training. You should consider the questions below before you make a decision to associate with a company:

- How many types of training sessions does the company provide?
- What is the level of commitment a company management places on training?
- Are the trainers qualified to train?
- How often does the company offer orientation training and product training?
- Does the company have the latest system of training?
- Does the trainer have the skills to make the audience laugh?
- Is the trainer well-aware of everything that he or she is required to know as far as his or her field of specialization is concerned?

Network Marketing companies must put significant stress on training because it is one of the most crucial areas that determine how far the distributors will get in the business.

Key points

1. Choosing the right company is like finding a good wife. If you marry the wrong person, then you should be ready to go through hell.
2. The right company is defined by the products and compensation plan.

Chapter 5: Building a Customer-Focused Selling

Have you ever tirelessly worked in your Network Marketing opportunity for longer than three months, talked to hundreds of potential clients, but still you didn't achieve the result you wanted? Well, what could be the secret that you need to do and experience significant results?

Yes! Effective network marketing requires that you become a salesperson. But, they once told you that you don't need to be a salesperson. They only said, "Simply go and share the products with as many people you can and help them learn to do the same!" Well, it sounds like they did make it sound very simple. So you are sitting there wondering why they would have to lie? They should have told you the exact truth. Well, it might be that they were saying the truth. Or it could be that they weren't aware that they were lying. They are professionals. Why would they not be aware of it? They were very successful in their time! But, still, you don't believe that. Is it possible for someone to be very good at something but not even tell it? Well, the answer is that most people don't realize what effective selling means.

Now, who is a true salesperson? Going even deeper, what is "Sales"? First, we are going to see what is not Sales.

- Sales isn't speaking with someone so that they can eventually purchase something that they didn't need. That legendary person you have heard about that can sell wine to a non-alcohol person is not a true salesperson. We call him a hustler who wants just to force anything upon you.

- Sales is not applying high-pressure tricks so that you convince people to buy something against their desire or will. Any person who does this is called a hustler.

Sales

Well, let's turn our attention and see what Sales is. First, we look at one of the best definition of sales that I like to use.

"That process of helping a potential buyer decide whether a given service offered or product offered for sale will fulfill their pre-existing desires and needs, and thereby make it easy for them to purchase."

We are going to break this definition so that we understand it better.

The Prospective buyer

We all buy products every day, sometimes from a "Salesperson," but often we buy from people that are selling, and we even never come to discover it. What makes us be a prospective buyer for a given product or service offering is the notion that we want the product offered. Also, you can identify a prospect by checking whether that product or service shall fulfill their need.

Product or service being offered

Always remember this for the rest of your life. You never buy a product because you want the product. You buy it because of what you believe the product is going to offer you. Let me use an example to explain this. When you see a beautiful long-sleeved shirt outside, what always comes to your mind first? If you are like me, you will say this in your head: "Damn it! Look at that beautiful long-sleeved shirt! I know I will look very smart in it!" As you can see you start to imagine how you will look when dressed in the shirt. This way, the shirt will make you look smart. If you were to walk to the shop and purchase the shirt, it is because you believe it will make you look very smart.

I realized that no one wants more money. What did I just say? Oh! Don't just believe it! Money is just a fancy paper with some ink on it. What most people focus on are the things that money can bring for them or do for them. And they will never buy a fridge to put on display.

They buy it because they want to preserve some of their home products. They want the end result. Once you can tell the desired result of a person, you are able to tell whether what you are providing will help them and hence determine whether they can be potential customers for your service or product.

Make it simple and easy to buy

To become a new customer, the potential customer has to make that decision to buy. Now, for you to be hopeful of succeeding, they must be ready to buy from you. If he does come and purchase it from you, it is because they believe your solution will provide them the desired result compared to other existing solutions they might have considered. Buying always turns to be very easy when obstacles encountered on the way are solved. You can always achieve this if you take time to describe your product or service in a manner that seems to go hand-in-hand with their needs.

Being social and friendly is important. It's never difficult, but you just need some practice and a genuine interest to help people solve their problem and get out of life what they are looking for. Do you now see why focusing on your desires first will result in failure? Success in NWM requires that your needs come second and the prospect's needs take the lead. And that is what we call effective selling!

To ensure that creating a customer-focused selling approach becomes easy, here is a memory aid for 7 roles of selling.

7 roles of Selling

1. The Student

Being a student, you must study the way changes influence your prospects and find avenues where you can add value. If you want to make larger and profitable sales that will help you become rich, you must look for bigger and considerable needs that you can fulfill.

2. The Doctor

Your duty as a doctor is to ask questions that will help you diagnose your potential customer's needs. If you're going to find them unsatisfied with their present living conditions, it indicates that they don't deserve to be where they are now. As a doctor, you have another role in identifying the complications that are most likely going to arise if they aren't going to resolve their discontent.

3. The Architect

Here, you have the responsibility to be innovative and develop unique solutions that are going to simplify your future potential customer research steps. Simplify for the intangible concepts so that they look more definite.

4. The Coach

While your prospect takes time to compare what you are offering to that of your market competitors, your goal as a coach is to beat your competitors without lowering the price. As a coach, you need to gain a competitive edge through insight and analysis. After that, you implement a winning strategy.

The steps that will assist you to grab that victory include:

- Design a game strategy that will help you positively position yourself against the competition.

- Assess your strengths and weaknesses and compare to those of your opponents.

- Demonstrate your superiority in the market with a great presentation and sales proposal.

5. The Negotiator

Your goal here is to reach an agreement to open a relationship, but not to close the sale. Negotiation is basically a discussion to arrive at an agreement between two or more parties who share a similar interest.

Here are some highlights to consider while you negotiate:

- Get ready to negotiate by identifying some of the things you want to gain from the agreement.

- Request for commitment in a manner that is non-manipulative.

- Reach an agreement by determining the interests of our customer, areas of agreement, and developing a win-win solution.

6. The Teacher

When a customer finishes purchasing a product, the salesperson must help the customer understand clearly that the product's value has been met. The salesperson can be useful on both fronts through assuming the role of a teacher. First, in the customer-focused selling, whatever objectives you have agreed upon must be measurable and realistic. Second, once you have set the goals, you must fulfill and control your customer expectations as well as teach them ways to attain their objectives. The goal is to help your customer understand how they should use your service or product for their maximum benefit. The test for value confirms whether what you said you are offering is true.

7. The Farmer

Your role as a farmer is to create the satisfaction as well as grow the account. Nowadays, companies that aim to be the best in the market have highlighted customer satisfaction in their key business strategy. To survive and succeed, you must remain very close to your customers, not only during the sales process but even after you are finished. Your customers will develop a certain perception of satisfaction based on several factors: Product quality, value achieved, price, and the quality of the service. One of the greatest worries with many salespeople is that the customers can be satisfied today. However, their opinion might come to change either tomorrow or someday. Building a good relationship has an advantage of generating more benefits down the road.

The Art of Making Presentations

Jeff Olson once said that having good presentation skills can deliver more for your career than having a collection of degrees from prestigious universities. Learning how to make effective presentations to your potential customers is one of the best things that will help your company expand. The top three presentation formats that you can apply include two-on-one, open meetings, and small group meetings.

Two-On-Ones

This presentation is called a two-on-one because you perform the presentation by partnering with a new person in your downline, for your potential customer. Two-On-Ones should be carried out at the home of the prospect or their office because if you are going to invite someone to come to your home or office, the stakes are high they might not turn up.

In achieving a thriving business in NWM, many successful network marketing companies got it through two-on-one presentations. This presentation technique comes with the following advantages:

- You can design your presentation based on the interests, age, experience, educational background and needs of the prospect.

- When you are giving a presentation, your downline partner has the opportunity to learn from your experience, so this presentation benefits both the prospect and your downline partner.

- It is very easy to deal with misconceptions, questions, and any other concerns. You can also deal with an objection by assigning the time and information required to deal with it. Unlike in a general meeting where you will require to reply with a general answer.

- While you give the presentation to one individual, he or she gets that pressure to make a decision right away even if you are not going to exert any pressure on him or her.

Small Group Meetings

Another great way of making a presentation is a small group meeting, often arranged at home. This is where someone new in your organization invites colleagues, friends or relatives to visit his or her home to see your presentation. While you invite people, don't forget that one negative person can ruin other people's interests. To avoid such situations:

- Don't invite prospects that seem negative when taking your call.

- At the start of the presentation, you can let your visitors know that if they have questions to ask in the middle of the presentation, they should wait until after the presentation to ask.

- If you see a person who constantly maintains negativity during the presentation, then you can request the host to transfer the guest into a separate room.

Open Meetings

Open meetings involve a certified professional with great experience in public speaking does a presentation to between 10–10,000 people in an auditorium or large hall.

Steps to follow to give an effective Network Marketing Presentation

Well, I believe that you are now aware of the best three methods you can apply to give a presentation, but that is not enough. You must also understand why giving the best presentation is important. Here are seven steps to follow to give an effective presentation.

1. **Maintain your individuality**

Have you ever been to a large audience and got the time to watch someone on stage and wished you were like that person? What do they seem to have that you don't? Do they appear to know all the answers? Do you want to know how you can just be like them? Truth be told. You can't. That is a common mistake that nearly each one of us makes at one point or another. You can emulate their success, but you will never be like them. To achieve success, you must be ready to let out your real you to manifest.

Most of the times in NWM, we have our mentors. They influence our lives, but the one thing you should never forget is to retain your individuality. That is your life signature. No one else can be like that. So always maintain your individuality.

2. **Have a presentation manual**

While you are giving a presentation to potential clients, you need to have with you a professional presentation document that you can demonstrate to the prospect—something visual while you are doing the presentation. A presentation document will save you the time of memorizing what you need to go and say.

3. **Your story**

Always make sure that you begin your presentation with your story. This is very effective in helping your prospects see you as a kind of person that they need to identify themselves with. Your story should not be very long, but make sure it is very captivating. It should carry the following three parts

- Your Why
- Your Background
- Your goals as well as ambitions

4. **Background of the company**

It is advisable that once you are through with letting the prospect know your story, spend another 4-5 minutes to talk about the company you are working with. You can cover the following in the company background:

- How long has the company been in operation, and where can it be found?
- What products or services does the company market, and how is their distribution network structured?
- Who are the company owners?
- What were the projected company's sales last year? Have they set realistic goals for this year?
- Highlight any award, recognition, or magazine articles that demonstrate the credibility of the company.
- Emphasize the type of training and support that your company seeks to offer to prospects right away.

5. Products and Services

The most key thing of a presentation is to present the services and products that your company is selling. Remember, most people who pay attention to your presentation will never run the business very aggressively the way you do, but they all have that chance to be potential customers. Some of the key things you should stress upon during this presentation include:

- If you didn't make any money in this business, still you would continue using the products and services each month because of their quality, low-cost and convenience.

- The products and services represent the cornerstone of the business opportunity.

Product presentation calls that you demonstrate how the products are of the highest quality.

Here are points to consider:

- Are the products environmentally safe?
- How unique are your products compared to your competitors'?
- Do the products have a patent or are manufactured by the company?
- Has any reputable agency done a quality assessment test on your products?
- Can your company's product be delivered to your prospect's residence in 3–4 business days?
- Do you have any personal testimonies to demonstrate that your products are of high quality?

6. Compensation Plan

This is the part where you can excite the prospect by disclosing the company residual income. Regardless of how your compensation plan appears, you must first remember to explain what residual income is. Most people aren't familiar with that term. Once you are through with it, you can then proceed to describe your company compensation plan.

7. Closing

When ending your presentation, you want to get a positive response from the questions you are going to ask such as: Would you want to be a customer or do the business? You don't want to end with a question that will give a negative response. For instance, don't end by asking, do you want to take part in this business or not? This is called the yes-no close. What would you do if they say no? Be creative and ask questions such as what part of the presentation excited you most? Or what did you like from the presentation?

Their answer doesn't really matter. Regardless of what the prospect says, you should respond by acknowledging, "Great! In that case, let me ask you a few questions."

Top 10 Proven tips in Network Marketing

1. Believe in your products, services, industry, company and your people.

2. The 90:10 secret. It states that 10% of life consists of what happens to you. You have no control over that. However, 90% of life is you who determines it through your reaction to it.

3. Make use of your abilities. Did you know that you miss about 100% of shots that you never take?

4. Accept your responsibilities.

5. Make use of your time. An anonymous Tibetan Monk once said that if you want to see your past, just look into your present life condition. If you would like to see your future, just observe your present life actions. Time is the greatest equalizer in the universe. Make use of it wisely.

6. Develop teamwork. Remember that you can succeed best by first helping others succeed.

7. Have a vision of where you want to go and reach in your Network Marketing business.

8. Have the right dedication and commitment. Commitment will translate a promise into a reality.

9. Stay persistent. Persistence is the difference between those who succeed and those who never do.

10. Develop a culture of reading. Stephen R. Covey once said that the primary key to success is developing a life-long reading culture.

Key points

1. A customer-focused selling will give you more opportunities in Network Marketing.

2. To build an effective customer-focused selling, you must assume the seven roles.

3. Mastering and practicing the art of presentation earns you prospects.

4. Top 10 Proven tips for success in Network Marketing.

Chapter 6: Lessons from A Network Marketing Millionaire

If you are among the people who think that you can attain massive success by having a home run swing or by hiring a few top leaders, then you are lost. That is not how it really works. Brian Carruthers suggests that one should not to think of getting those big deals. Brian says, "You build your massive empire one block at a time." Consuming seven apples at once on a Sunday doesn't make you healthy. Instead, it is the "an apple a day" that will build and improve your health. The idea is to remain consistent when it comes to eating.

According to Brian Carruthers, his mentor whispered to him that "a two-a-day and a weekly meeting" are the formulae that will give you success. The concept of success in network marketing business is to ensure that you expose new people to your product and business opportunity. So you will agree with me that if you are not taking actions to expose many new, different people in your business, there is no hope that your business will grow big, right?

Brian goes on to suggest that you must be ready to spark the interest of new prospects so that they take a look at your presentation. Well, in this chapter I will walk you through the lessons of Brian Carruthers in Network Marketing.

Let's start with the two-a-day concept

The "two-a-day" formula is all about getting two people each day to take a look at a presentation. The great thing about this is that your company has the required resources to make this attainable for those people who might not have the time to do a 1-2 hour meetings every day.

The concept behind this formula is that anyone in the company can submit two tools that they can request people to review when they return home. Since the internet has revolutionized the marketing industry, people can simply send an email with a link to a video or even an audio for review. The point is to get two people every day and let them review a presentation tool, then you can follow up with answer questions and do a 3-way call before you close.

So the question that you need to ask yourself is whether you believe that you can find two people each day. It doesn't matter the place. It can be a person you encounter at a gas station, sit next to while on the plane, your Uber driver, or simply a new friend on social media.

For sure, you can do this. The question is "are you going to do it?" That can only be determined if you have the willpower. How motivating your "why" is determines your willpower. This means if your life was to depend on finding two new exposures each day, obviously you will have them done before 1:00 p.m. However, because many of the people who run a network marketing business don't place that level of priority on their business, most retire to bed every night without even exposing their business to two new people. In other words, these people don't consider their business success as a huge priority.

Make that choice to succeed

So let's assume that you want to attain success in network marketing. You are ready to dedicate to doing whatever you deem necessary to get that big win. Perhaps you are going to ask a few questions such as "what is the goal with the daily exposures?" Are you ready to do two exposures every day? That is workable from a time dedication angle, right?

So you have started doing it every day. How should you do it? Someone might ask that question. There is no defined formula. Just do it loudly. By that I mean let your entire team get to know that you are doing them. You can post your daily exposures, speak about with your friends, share it with your friends. Just become obsessed with the two-a-day.

Next is influencing others to emulate you. Think about if you are going to get five recruits to do the same. And so they copy everything, and we now have five recruits

each doing the same. Have a look at what that will translate to in the table below:

You x 2 = 2	2 exp. a day!	(60 x 5% = 3 recruits/month)
5 x 2 = 10	12 exp. a day!	(360 x 5% = 18 recruits/month)
25 x 2 = 50	62 exp. a day!	(1860 x 5% = 93 recruits/month)
125 x 2 = 250	312 exp. a day!	(9360 x 5% = 468 recruits/month)
625 x 2 =1250	1562 exp. a day!	(46,860 x 5% = 2343 recruits/month)

You can see from the above table that your two-a-day might not directly be the factor. However, it is the hundreds of people that will emulate you that will generate millions.

You are the Key

Let's now assume that you have done what I have briefly described, and you are now reaping the fruits. Well, take note. If you're going to stop doing it, then your team is going to notice, and soon the momentum is going to go down. Eventually, no one will be doing it. Your leaders are going to stop the same way you stopped. And so their leaders will also stop. Therefore, it is very important that you continue to lead a good example because you are the one with the key to life. Even if you feel that nobody is watching you, they are. The unnoticed universe forces shall disclose the truth.

Keeping it real

When it comes to the two-a-day exposures, keeping it real is very crucial. Let's say you have gone full-time and you are now doing between 10–20 a day. That is good for you. But don't talk about this to your business team because it can seem very overwhelming, and don't forget that the majority are part-timers.

The power of networking

Finally, remember that network marketing isn't about you doing all the work alone. No! That was a traditional business. Network marketing is about many people each fulfilling a certain task. It is about exponential growth through emulation. And emulation happens in every individual network marketing business. Unfortunately, most people duplicate a person that is not doing the work, and they end up failing.

Key points

1. Two-a-day is the secret strategy to success in Network Marketing.
2. Every network marketer should aim to improve the exposure of their business.

Conclusion

Thank for making it through to the end of *The 1000 Men Strong Leader*. Let's hope it was informative and able to provide you with all of the tools you need to achieve your goals whatever they may be.

Network Marketing is about picking new opportunities, searching for new exposure, and choosing a new financial future. Discover today why network marketing is being used by thousands of companies across the world to reach to consumers, and how you can use that opportunity to build a financially rewarding network marketing empire. The 1000 Men Strong Leader is an invaluable tool for both anyone looking forward to starting a career in network marketing or those looking to find solutions to why they aren't succeeding in Network Marketing. The book presents you with facts about the latest and hottest trend in the distribution and sales industry.

With plenty of information to help any person struggling to find the right path to network marketing, now is the perfect time for you to stop what you are doing and ask yourself—what do you really want to achieve in Network Marketing? Which areas are you going to concentrate on to build a Network Marketing empire? How ready are you to start building your career in Network Marketing?

Are you ready to execute the "two-a-day" strategy to improve your business exposure? By reading 'The 1000 Men Strong Leader,' you are proving that you are ready to seek out new and effective sources that will help improve or start your Network Marketing business. Remember that the most important type of investment is to invest in yourself.

Robert S. DeRopp once said that every man and woman should look, above all, a game that they can play. Once you find the game, play it with the passion as if your life and sanity relied on it. However, if life does not provide you with a game worth to play, then that is your chance to invent your game. He concludes by saying playing any game is better than not playing a game. Likewise, to succeed in the game of Network Marketing, you must be ready to play the game as if your life and sanity depend on it.

Description

Have you heard of Network Marketing? You haven't? Well, *The 1000 Men Strong Leader* is a unique Network Marketing book that seeks to help any person struggling in the Network Marketing profession or those looking to optimize their Network Marketing business. The book highlights deadly mistakes that many people in the network marketing industry make and further provides you with appropriate steps to take to solve these problems.

If you have been looking for a book that will help you realize your dream of building a Network Marketing Empire just like Brian Carruthers, then this is the book that you should aim to read. Written in a simple, interesting and engaging tone by a professional Network Marketer, *The 1000 Men Strong Leader* drives you through a journey where you can visualize and see with your eyes the way you can create your own stream of wealth in Network Marketing. Every word used in this book has been carefully chosen to help read easily and realize the many opportunities presented to you out there.

With plenty of actions to take and advice to follow, there is no room left for you to get it wrong when you start to build your network marketing empire. Most people fail to succeed in Network Marketing because of several reasons. Inside this book you are going to learn:

- How can you start and build a successful network marketing empire?

- Why are many network marketers struggling?

- Why only few network marketers succeed yet the opportunities are still many?

- Common misconceptions about Network Marketing.

- Who are prospects? How can you master the game of prospecting?

- Top 10 proven tips used by successful Network Marketers?

- What is customer-focused selling? How can you achieve a customer-focused selling in your company?

- The best most successful presentation technique for Network Marketers. How do you master the art of presentation?

- The four engines to help you select the right network marketing company.

- Lessons from a Network Marketing millionaire.

www.ingramcontent.com/pod-product-compliance
Lightning Source LLC
LaVergne TN
LVHW010435070526
838199LV00066B/6038